To order additional copies of this book, contact:
Xlibris
1-888-795-4274
www.Xlibris.com
Orders@Xlibris.com

ISBN: Softcover   978-1-7960-6841-2
         EBook   978-1-7960-6840-5

Print information available on the last page

Rev. date: 10/28/2019

This book is dedicated to my three children Donna-Marie, Destiny, and Anthony Jr., who all understand that life is full of endless possibilities if they are willing to TRY. And to all the smart, intelligent boys and girls across the world who are trying to do the best that they can in school.

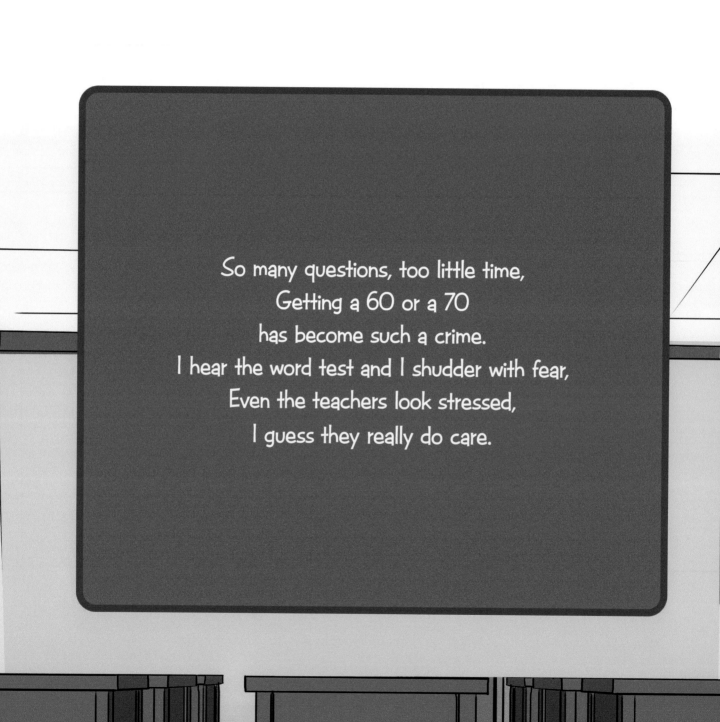

So many questions, too little time,
Getting a 60 or a 70
has become such a crime.
I hear the word test and I shudder with fear,
Even the teachers look stressed,
I guess they really do care.

I recall some test tips that my teacher taught well,
Read the question! Underline key words! Now ring a bell.
Which one should I choose?
Is it A? Is it B?
A voice in my head saying:" Choose the best answer you see."

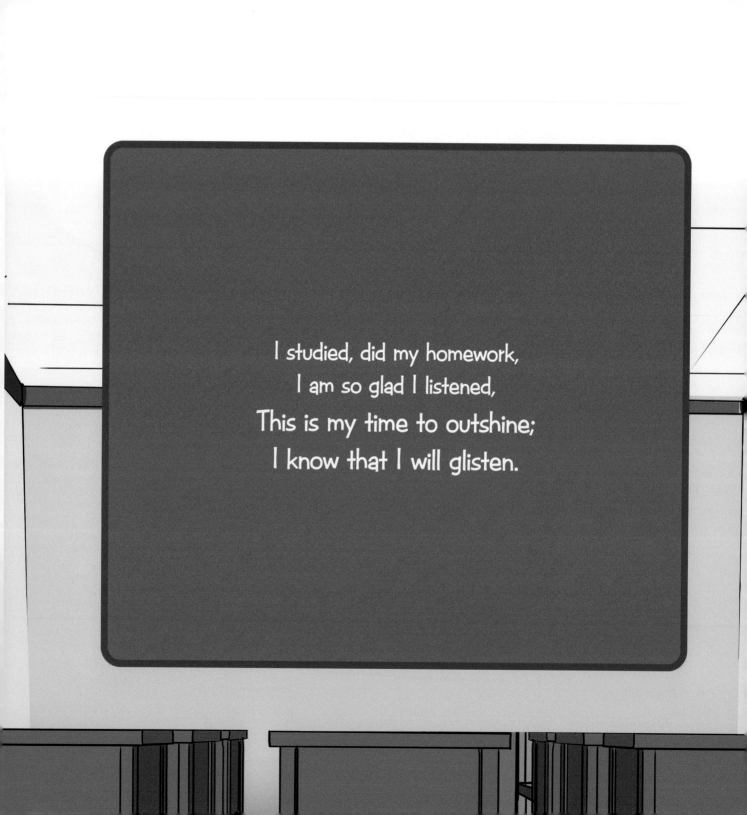

I have heard the word test now for so many days;
we practiced and practiced in so many ways.
I don't like this pressure;
I don't want to fail.
Oh wait! I know these answers,
we practiced them well.

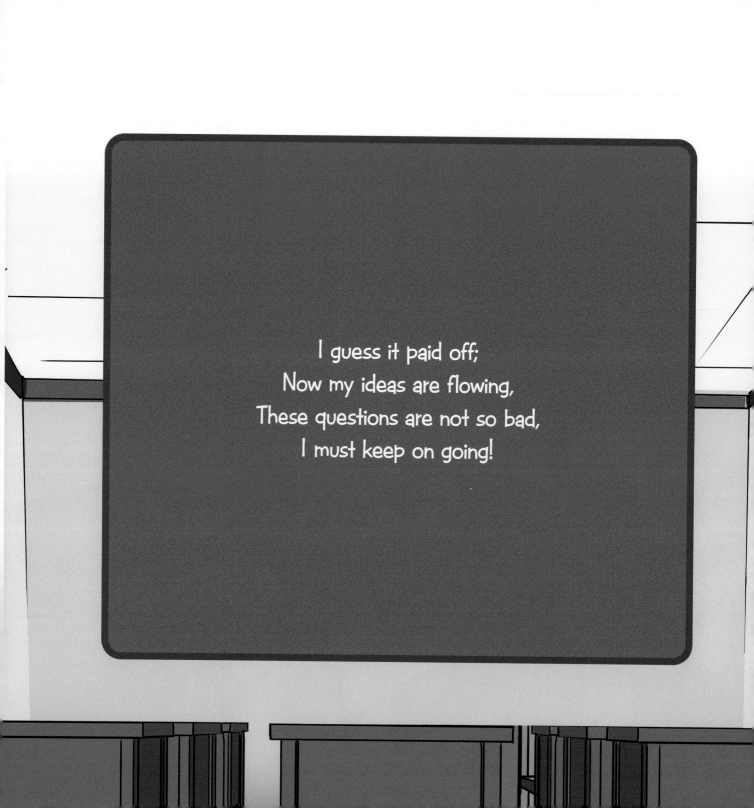

A teacher once said that a test is nothing but a show,
So I am going to show-off and expose what I know.

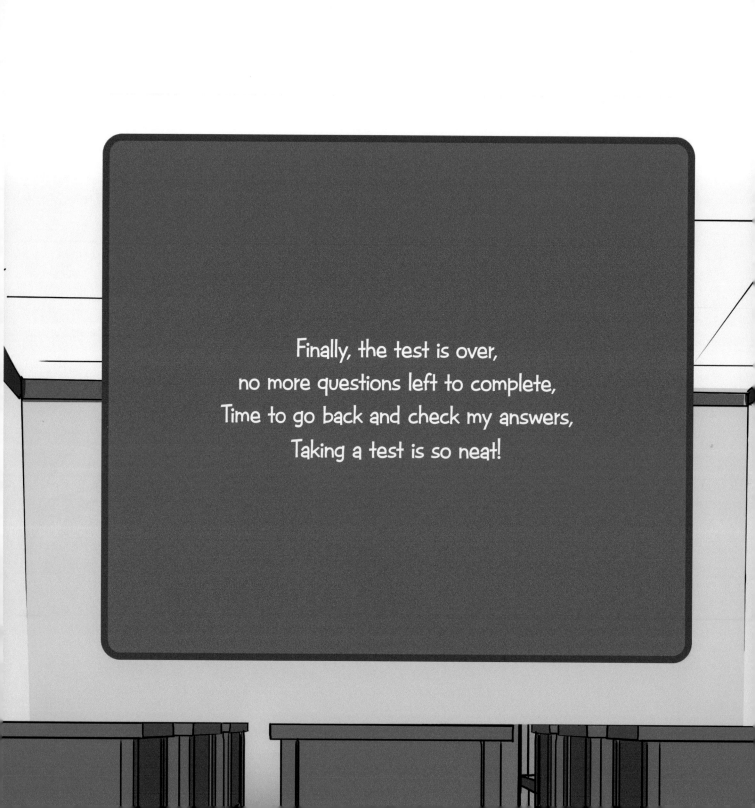

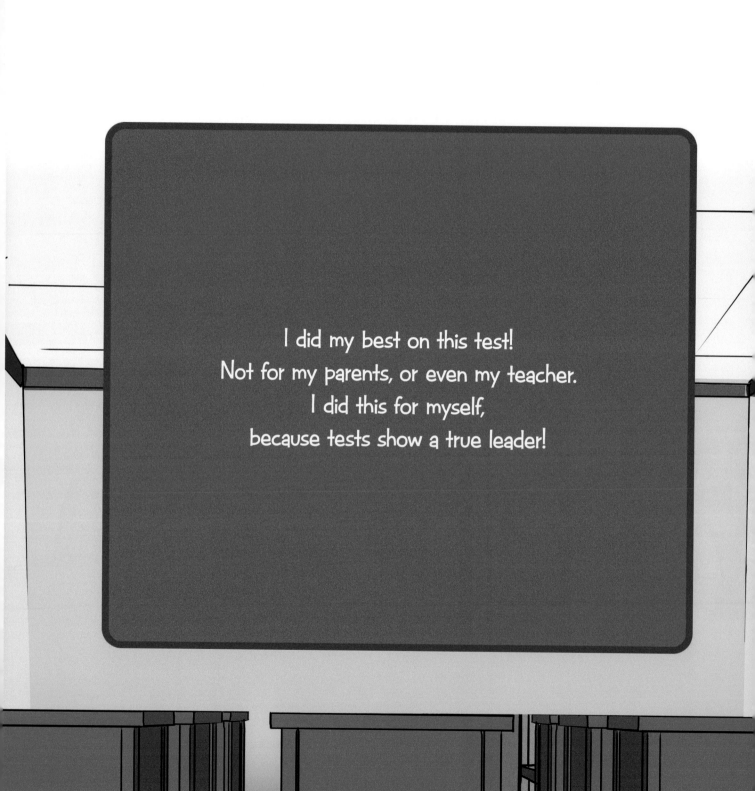

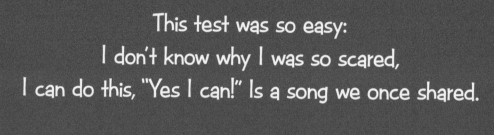

This test was so easy:
I don't know why I was so scared,
I can do this, "Yes I can!" Is a song we once shared.

Oh No, Not another test are my words no more,
I will say:" Come on! Bring it on!
I have so much to show!"

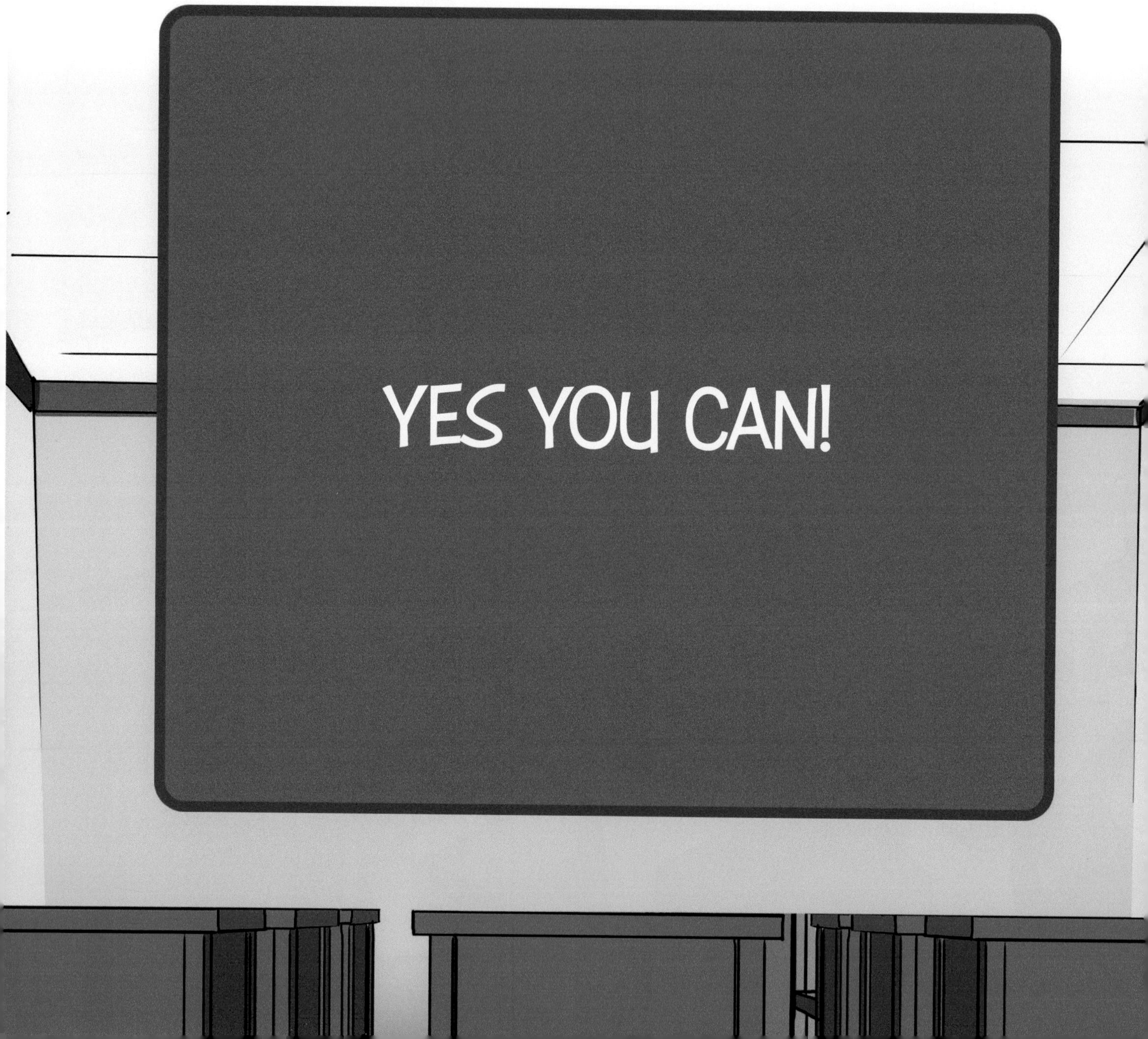
YES YOU CAN!

TEST-TAKING PREPARATION TIPS

› Get a good night's rest before the day of the test. Go to bed early.
› Eat a good healthy breakfast on the day of the test.
› Prepare yourself by completing all homework assignments, studying, and paying attention in class.
› Stay calm and positive .Remind yourself that a test is like a talent show, a time to "show off" what you already know.
› Speak positive words to yourself: Tell yourself that you CAN do this.
› Pray, meditate, and believe in yourself.

Printed in the United States
By Bookmasters